I0003664

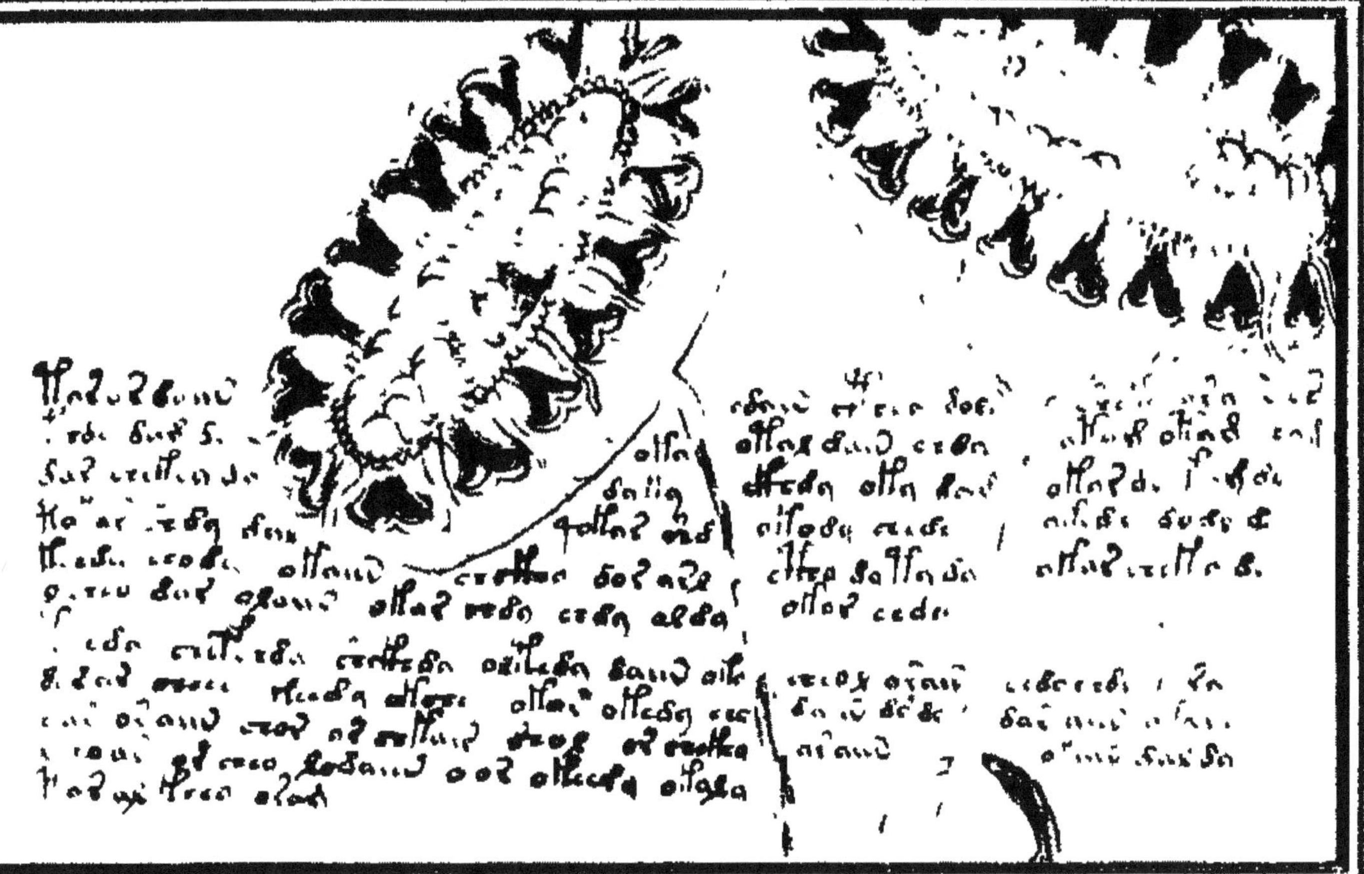

NEW RESEARCH ON THE VOYNICH MANUSCRIPT

Proceedings of a Seminar

30 November 1976

Washington, D. C.

NEW RESEARCH ON THE VOYNICH MANUSCRIPT

PROCEEDINGS OF A SEMINAR

30 November 1976

Washington, D.C.

CONTENTS

FIGURES

EDITORIAL PREFACE

These notes contain the proceedings of a one-day seminar on the Voynich manuscript, held in Washington, DC, on 30 November 1976. With the exception of Dr. Fairbanks' presentation (of which he provided a written version for inclusion in these proceedings), all the material was transcribed by me, with only minor editing, from a taped record of the sessions. I apologize in advance to those speakers during the discussion period who could not be identified (because I could not recognize their voices on the tape). I apologize also to anyone whose comments I may have inadvertently omitted, or who feels that his remarks may not have been transcribed correctly. I hope that these notes will serve as a faithful and valuable record of this seminar, and of the many interesting and important methodological points that were raised during the discussions.

M. E. D'Imperio

I.A. General Introduction. Vera Filby, Sponsor.

Good morning, and welcome to our seminar on the Voynich manuscript. A year ago this month, Brigadier Tiltman, who is here with us today in the front row, gave a talk on the Voynich manuscript - the most mysterious manuscript in the world. This talk so inspired two of our members that they have since engaged in serious research into the problem, within the rather considerable range of their own specialities: cryptanalysis in the one case and linguistics in the other. I knew of their work, and was keeping up with it, and it seemed to me that with reports on their research, the Voynich would again make an appropriate topic for a program. It seemed to me that there is never likely to be a better collection of the right kind of brains, talent, and training than we have right here and right now, and so I proposed this seminar. The history of attempts to break the "Cipher Manuscript" (as Wilfrid M. Voynich himself called it) has been a history of frustrations and even disasters, but maybe we can strike the right spark today; maybe we can open up the first real cracks.

I would certainly be proud if our initiative were to make such a contribution to the scholarly world; but if that is too sanguine a hope, we have the more modest wish that Mrs. Friedman offered in her letter to me a few days ago in response to my invitation to her to attend. She didn't feel well enough to come, but she did write, and she said, "Greetings to all of you, and may you be crowned with, at least, a glimmer of hope." And maybe that's the best that we can really expect.

Now Ladies and Gentlemen, it is my pleasure to introduce our moderator for the Voynich seminar, Miss Mary D'Imperio. Mary is in the final stages of completing a monograph on the history of research on the Voynich manuscript; she calls it "The Elegant Enigma." It is, I think, a magnificently scholarly job, and eventually you'll all have a chance to read it. Mary has degrees in Comparative Philology and Classics from Radcliffe, and Structural Linguistics from the University of Pennsylvania. Her career has been with the Government since 1951. She is a linguist and cryptanalyst, but she thinks of herself mainly as a computer programmer, and it is this combination of talents that makes her so right for the enterprise that she and the other participants in the seminar will undertake today. There can't be, I think, anyone better equipped anywhere to take on the job that she's about to do, which is to lead this enquiry into the search for solutions to the mystery of the Voynich manuscript.

I.B. Introductory Remarks. M. E. D'Imperio, Moderator.

Before I present our featured speakers, I would like to give a brief introduction, for the benefit of those who may be unfamiliar with the problem of the Voynich manuscript. My remarks will center around two main topics: first, I will try to sketch, very rapidly, something of the history and physical nature of the manuscript. Then, I want to say something about the cryptanalytic problem posed by the manuscript, and some of the things that have made it so challenging and so interesting to so many people.

The Voynich manuscript itself has the shape of a small book, about nine inches long and six inches wide. Most pages contain colored pictures of plants and astronomical or astrological diagrams. Here are some slides showing some sample pages so you can get an idea of what they are like. (It was, unfortunately, not possible to reproduce the slides here. -Ed.) Some seem to be medical or pharmaceutical in nature, and feature naked human figures, mostly female. These figures have very plump and matronly shapes, and appear to be sitting, standing, or swimming amid a weird conglomeration of tubs, pipes, and other odd plumbing. No one, as far as I know, has gotten very far in figuring out what any of the pictures mean.

On almost every page, there is a lot of writing in brownish ink. It is very fluent, clear, and relatively neat, but it is in a writing system that nobody has, so far, been able to identify with any known language or culture.

The Voynich manuscript was discovered in 1912 by Wilfrid M. Voynich, a rare book dealer. He found it at the Villa Mondragone, near Rome, among other manuscripts which he was buying in a large lot. With it was a letter, dated 1665 or 1666, from a man named Joannus Marcus Marci to Athanasius Kircher, a well-known Jesuit scholar with a strong interest in cryptology. Marci was a scholar associated with the court of the Emperor Rudolph the Second in Prague. The letter said that Marci was giving the mysterious manuscript to Kircher, in the hope that he would be able to decipher it. The letter also said that the manuscript was thought to be by Roger Bacon, a philosopher of the thirteenth century in whose work there was great interest at Rudolph's court at the time.

Several people have claimed that they could read the cipher in modern times. The most famous solution was that of Professor William R. Newbold in 1921, which was completely demolished by Professor John Manly of the University of Chicago in 1931. Mr. and Mrs. William F. Friedman also had a part in the research which resulted in the disproof of Newbold's claim.

Since that time, although there have been several other claims to a solution, none has succeeded in convincing cryptologists or any other scholars that the mystery has really been solved. The elegant puzzle is still there today, waiting for all of us to try our hand.

The manuscript itself remained in the possession of Mr. Voynich, and after his death, in his wife's estate. It was purchased in 1961 by H. P. Kraus, another antiquarian bookseller, for the sum of $24,500 in cash. He tried to sell it, reputedly for as much as $100,000 and later $160,000, but apparently couldn't find a buyer. In 1969, he presented it to the Beinecke Rare Book Library of Yale University, where it now is.

Now, I would like to say a few words about the analytic problems presented by the Voynich manuscript. Why is it such a persistent and fascinating problem? Why has no one succeeded in solving it in the nearly fifty-five years since its discovery?

First, nearly everything about the problem is an unknown. We don't know what country or even what part of the world the manuscript came from. We don't know what language underlies the text, or even if it is a natural language at all. We have no sure knowledge of the date of its origin, although most students agree it cannot be much earlier that 1450 or much later than 1550. As far as we can find out, no scientific study has ever been made of the vellum or the inks, and no paleographic studies have been made of the writing. We have no clue about who the author or authors could have been, or why they wrote it.

Attempts to discover other manuscripts with similar writing or drawings have been completely unsuccessful. The Voynich manuscript seems to be a unique document. We have had little or no success in figuring out what the pictures mean, or using them to break into the text. There is, in short, nothing that can serve as a crib or Rosetta Stone.

The scribe or scribes of the manuscript have been fanatically careful to leave nothing in the clear to give us a break-in point to the text. While there are a few scribbled phrases in other writings on some pages, they are so crabbed and faint that nobody has been able to make much out of them. They have never, so far as we can tell, been examined under special lighting or otherwise studied scientifically as they should be to see what, if anything, they do say.

On top of these very general difficulties, there are some basic analytic problems that hamper us in attacking the Voynich text. First there is the writing system or alphabet; we simply don't understand how it works. The symbols seem to be built up from smaller units in some way, but we can't come up with a convincing analysis into basic elements. So we don't really know how many letters there are in the alphabet; some students see as few as 17, while others see as many as 39. Each researcher has his own theory about the alphabet and his own transcription. Then there is the question of what the cipher units are and what plaintext units they represent. Are we dealing with words as wholes, syllables, mixed-length strings, or single letters? Finally, there are very few patterned repeats in the text that can give us a clue to the workings of the system. While many single word-like elements are copiously repeated throughout the text, we have had little success in finding any parallel elements in the context surrounding occurrences of similar groups.

There are approximately 250,000 characters of text in the manuscript. No one has apparently ever succeeded in completing a machine index or concordance of the entire corpus. For the most part, only small samples of 5,000 to 20,000 characters have been studied in any detail. A hand concordance was made by Father Petersen of Catholic University; unfortunately, this is with the Friedman collection in Lexington, Virginia, where it is not readily accessible to many students.

These are some of the reasons why the Voynich manuscript has been rightly called a Mount Everest for cryptographers by some, and a work of the Devil by others who have struggled in vain with its puzzles within puzzles.

Theories that have been held by various researchers concerning the nature of the Voynich text fall into the following five general categories:

First, some think the text is in a natural language, not enciphered or concealed deliberately in any way, but simply written in an unfamiliar script. Mr. Child's theory, which we will soon hear him describe, is based on this assumption.

Second, some maintain that the text is a form of natural language, but enciphered in some variety of simple substitution with various complicating factors. The theory of Dr. Robert S. Brumbaugh of Yale University, announced in 1974, is of this nature.

Third, some think the text is not in a natural language at all, but rather in a code or synthetic language like Esperanto, using an invented alphabet for further concealment. William F. Friedman was a proponent of this theory, and Brigadier Tiltman has also favored it.

Fourth, some believe the Voynich manuscript is an artificial fabrication, and much of the text is randomly-generated, meaningless padding. Within it there is some quantity of decipherable text. Dr. Brumbaugh also holds this view; he feels that the manuscript was manufactured in the sixteenth century by an opportunist for the specific purpose of peddling it to the Emperor Rudolph in Prague. According to this theory, while most of the text is meaningless and will never be read, some portions can be deciphered if we know how.

Fifth, there are some who believe that the text is all completely meaningless doodling, produced by a mentally-disturbed or eccentric person. According to this view, we will never make any sense out of it, no matter what we do. Doris Miller, a recently retired colleague who has returned to be with us today, has presented an eloquent case for this theory.

With this introductory sketch to set the stage, I will now introduce our first speaker.

James Child

Mr. Child received his A.B. in Germanic Languages and Literatures from Princeton University, and an M.A. in Baltic and Slavic Philology from the University of Pennsylvania. He has had a long and distinguished career as a linguist, both in the practical and theoretical aspects of the field. He has worked as a translator, has taught many basic language courses in a wide range of languages, and has been active in the design of language proficiency tests for job placement and career development. His interest in the Voynich manuscript was aroused by Brigadier Tiltman's lecture in November of last year. He has published two brief articles on his theory concerning the manuscript in periodicals circulated within his organization. We are happy to have Mr. Child here today to tell us of his approach to solving the mystery.

I.C. A Linguistic Approach to the Voynich Text. James Child.

I sincerely hope that my work doesn't go the way of poor Newbold, or Manly, who demolished Newbold's theory but didn't do any better himself. This seems to have been the case for anyone who has had the gall to get anything out of the manuscript: nobody comes out looking very good, but then nobody is put down permanently either. It is still an open case.

There is still a lot of work to be done, but I do believe I have an opening wedge into the manuscript. I feel that I know at least a few things about the nature of the underlying language, which I believe to be human language, plaintext, an Indo-European language, and a language in the Germanic family. Beyond that I would be rash in going.

Assuming this is a natural language, what kind of distribution would you get? First, you would expect words and characters to fall in certain positions. Finding a sequence of four or five letters, all of which you had assumed were vowels, occurring in a row would argue against a simple cipher. But if you find reasonable sequences of vowels interspersed among consonants, there would have to be a very sophisticated enciphering mechanism to produce such text if it were not in fact plaintext. In the Voynich text, I believe we have a complex situation: vowel letters, consonant letters, and digraphs. The digraphs occur especially at the ends of words, tending to obscure the grammatical relationships. I will elucidate further later on.

First, I'd like to give you a notion of the procedure I've followed in trying to break this text. A few definitions are in order: they are linguistic in nature, and I'll try to make them as painless as possible for those having an aversion to linguistics.

1. Morphemes. All languages have sound combinations that represent meaning units. At a lower level, a sound sequence is just a syllable, but at some level you begin to have potentially meaningful units. Nevertheless, meaning is always in context. I have tended to approach the Voynich in this way: what are the bases and affixes (prefixes, suffixes, and infixes), and do they seem sound and reasonable in terms of the particular sort of language I assume underlies the system? These units are morphemes: values lexically and semantically possible.

2. Lexemes. Lexemes are the same values, but in context. Scholars cannot immediately zero in on meanings of words when they are studying a new language. They try to find what the parts of speech are, how they relate to one another, the alignments of nouns and verbs, and so forth. For example, short words or morphemes occurring in front of noun-like things give you prepositions; words linking noun and verb combinations can be conjunctions; and so forth. Once you have nailed down some of these, you try to specify certain kinds of nouns (for example, the declensions in Indo-European languages). You try to refine the nouns and relate them to the things you are calling verbs, to establish, for example, a noun plural going with a third person plural verb form, etc. These are going to be lexemes: meanings of morphemes in particular contexts.

3. Sememes. Our final definition, that of the sememe, stands for the concept that the writer is trying to express and get across to the reader; the idea behind the forms (morphemes) and the forms in context (lexemes).

This is the theoretical approach I've used to attack this problem. I tried early on to establish, first of all, the letter patterns: the morphemes. I came to the conclusion that the morphemes I found were valid for a human language in the Indo-European family and in the Germanic family in particular, and that they seemed to play the proper role as lexemes.

(Could I have the first slide please? By the way, I want to thank Mary D'Imperio for doing these; my handwriting is absolutely abysmal in my native script, so far be it from me to take on the Voynich!) (See Fig 1.a.) One of the first things I noticed was this place at the top of the slide, from folio 114, which has "OOR." If that could be considered a way of lengthening the "O," the word would be a good preposition in the North Germanic language family. The next group after that would have to be a noun by definition; what kind of a noun, Heaven only knows. But I could add the information that the preposition "OOR" would require the dative case. The final letter of that next word is a consonant in my reconstruction: either "D" or (the sound at the beginning of the English word "the" -Ed.), so it's not a dative ending. It could be a feminine noun with a zero ending - possible for some North Germanic languages. The next group, which I read as "OG," is still the conjunction "and" in most Scandinavian languages. It appears in other Germanic languages as "auch," "also," (although the word for "and" in West Germanic is either "and" or "und"). This suggested tentatively establishing the language as North Germanic. Here you have a preposition, a noun, and a conjunction, so you need another noun, to give you something like "From ---- and ----."

This approach gives the whole thing an extremely algebraic appearance. In English, if you did the same thing, and left out all the content words, keeping only the function words (like "the," "of," "and," etc.) and the inflexions (the "-ing's" and "-s's" and "-ed's"), you would get something like this: "(Somebody or something) is doing, will do, or did do (something) to (someone) at or in (some place)." You, the listener, may regard this as absolutely idiotic, and in terms of a message, of course it is. But in terms of the informational process it is not at all meaningless, and is in fact quite instructive. You have, in fact, to reconstruct something or this sort when you are working with an unknown language, to prove, or at least to suggest strongly, that you've got a real language. Taking words out of context, by themselves, obviously won't do.

Now on the second part of this slide (Fig 1.b.) we see a repeat of the conjunction "OG." In front of it we have a word I assume to be "THOR" or "TOR." That letter at the beginning could stand for "TH" or "T"; this sort of thing was most common in German manuscripts. Old High German is a living horror; in ways much worse than the Voynich: you can have eight or nine different spellings for words or names. So the fact that the first letter of

"THOR" may be "T" as well as "TH" doesn't bother me very much.

After the "OG," it looks as if we might have a parallel noun; perhaps another god, or simply another man's name, depending on who "Thor" actually was. I thought this might be "THRUTHER." Thruther is, in some legends, the daughter of Thor, in others simply the hammer of Thor. It would seem a good guess to try to reconstruct morphemes and put more lexemes in, so I went on that assumption. Incidentally, the first word here, "FRIBĀ," looks very reasonable to me; the "R" doesn't look like a final "R," because it's apparently a digraph: "R" plus short vowel "E" or "I." That equation holds up pretty well through the pages I've studied. I've given some consideration to nine or ten different pages; I haven't just stuck with one, which would be foolish.

Obviously, I wanted to look beyond simple noun collocations. I wanted to see if I could find some parallel syntax. In slide two (See Fig 1.c.), we have what appears to be a repeat of "THOR," and the second word I regard as "LIŌFĀ," which would mean "beloved." We have a possible genitive plural with long "Ā" for the third word - a correct Scandinavian genitive plural. A repeat of "OG," "and," run together with "THOR"; more often than not the conjunction is run together with the following word. The first word in the second line may be read as "ĀLIĀ," "nourisher, he who nourishes." We would have to assume a Norse participial form for that. But that's rather shaky, and I'm quite dubious about it.

Down in line 18 (Fig 1.d.), I've tried to extend my procedure a little further. Those underlinings are adjective and noun. Incidentally, the noun plural forms (and I think I've isolated four different noun plural forms in this language) match Swedish very closely, better than any of the other Scandinavian languages (although my original assumption had been Danish). It seems indeed to be closer to a form of Swedish, but it's not pure Swedish either. I have conjectured - and this is a simple conjecture, nothing more - that what we may have here is a residue of Gothic; not the language of the Goths of Bishop Ulfilas' time in the fourth century, but the latter-day Goths, those people who settled Southern Sweden and parts of Northern Denmark. This may, perhaps, be their dialect. I don't know for sure - I just want to make a suggestion.

In slide three, at the top (Fig 1.e.), we have another nominative plural noun, then we have a plural third person form. The third person plural ending is usually "-Ā," so this, I'm assuming, may be "-N̄Ā." That final digraph "-N̄Ā" holds up pretty well in many places. So we have something like this: "These people or things, whatever they are, do something, whatever it is they do." Again, this is admittedly algebraic, but nevertheless, this is the procedure I followed. The bottom example on this slide (Fig 1.f.), has another nominative plural of a noun, then our conjunction "OG," then "THĀ," which is a good Norse demonstrative, and goodness knows what that last word is.

We'll go on to the last slide, and I'll try to wind up here. (Fig 1.g.) We have the first two words in this line repeated over and over again on some of the pages I've studied. I'm reading them "GOTTAR REĪÐĀ." "Gottar" would be "the Goths." That, incidentally, would be the Swedish nominative plural today. "Reíðā," again a third person plural form, is perfectly correct: the digraph for "RE," then long "Ī," the "θ" letter again, which is our "Þ"; "REĪÞĀ," like German "reden," "to say or pronounce." "And the Goths say..." I'm not sure what the next word - "GOTTEÞA" - is, but the last two words could be "ΟF LATAIN," "in Latin," and then "RES ĀLMĀ." "Res alma" is not a very good co-occurrence in Latin; it's perfectly good grammatically. I don't know about it as a phrase; it might mean a "charitable thing," or a "good thing."

All of these examples are intended to be primarily an illustration of the method. A lot of these findings are obviously still going to be in doubt for some time, but I'm having a lot of fun with it! I think if you don't have fun doing something like this, a lot of the purpose is lost. I certainly appreciate everybody here coming to listen to my ramblings, and I guess we'll see a great number of you this afternoon at the later session.

Thank you very much.

a. Folio 114r, line 2:

OOR OG

FROM AND

b. Folio 40v, lines 9, 10:

FRIDĀ THOR OG THRUTHAIR

THOR AND THRUTHER

c. Folio 58r, line 1:

THOR LIBFĀ OTHOR ĀLIĀ

THOR BELOVED (GEN. PL.) AND THOR NOURISHER(?)

d. Folio 58r, line 18:

(ADJ.) (N. PL.) NOUN

e. Folio 58r, line 21:

(N. PL.) NOUN (3 PL.) VERB

f. Folio 58r, line 22:

OGTHĀ

(N. PL.) NOUN AND (DEMONST. PL.)

g. Folio 107v, lines 10, 11:

GOTTAR REIDĀ GOTTIDĀ OF LATAIN RES ĀLMĀ

GOTHS SAY "GOTTIDA", IN LATIN "RES ALMA".

Fig. 1. Sample Readings (Mr. Child)

Voynich Symbol	Equivalent
o	ŏ
oo	ō
a	ă
9	ā
ai	ĕ (ai)
c	ĭ
cc	u or m
a	ī
4	g
ℓ	gh (as consonant) (after vowels, lengthens vowel)
ꝗ, ꞁ	t, th (as in thing)
8	d, ð (as in the)
[illegible], [illegible]	p
[illegible], [illegible]	f
ꝛ	r
ƨ	s
ɔ	n, or n + short vowel
cɾ	li
cɾ (with 2 above)	ri
ɟ	is
⋏	? (possibly a Greek sound χ)

Fig. 2. Symbol Correspondences (Mr. Child)

Captain Prescott H. Currier (USN Ret.)

Captain Currier received an A.B. in Romance Languages at George Washington University, and a Diploma in Comparative Philology at the University of London. He began his cryptologic career in 1935, and was called to active duty with the Navy in 1940. He has served in many distinguished capacities in the field, and from 1948 to 1950, was Director of Research, Naval Security Group. Since his retirement in 1962, he has continued to serve as a consultant. His interest in the Voynich manuscript has been of very long standing, and he has devoted an impressive amount of rigorously scientific analytic effort to the problem in recent years. We are fortunate indeed that Captain Currier has consented to come from his lovely home in Maine to speak to us today about his research.

I.D. Some Important New Statistical Findings. Capt. Prescott Currier.

I will start out by saying that I don't have any "solution." I have a succession of what I consider to be rather important facts which I would like to review briefly. The two most important findings that I think I have made are the identification of more than one hand and the identification of more than one "language." The reason they are important is that, if this manuscript were to be considered a hoax as it is by some, it's much more difficult to explain this if you consider that there was more than one individual involved, and that there is more than one "language" involved. These findings also make it seem much less likely that the manuscript itself is meaningless.

Two Hands and Two "Languages" in the Herbal Section. When I first looked at the manuscript, I was principally considering the initial (roughly) fifty folios, constituting the herbal section. The first twenty-five folios in the herbal section are obviously in one hand and one "language," which I called "A." (It could have been called anything at all; it was just the first one I came to.) The second twenty-five or so folios are in two hands, very obviously the work of at least two different men. In addition to this fact, the text of this second portion of the herbal section (that is, the next twenty-five of thirty folios) is in two "languages," and each "language" is in its own hand. This means that, there being two authors of the second part of the herbal section, each one wrote in his own "language." Now, I'm stretching a point a bit, I'm aware; my use of the word language is convenient, but it does not have the same connotations as it would have in normal use. Still, it is a convenient word, and I see no reason not to continue using it.

"Languages" A and B Statistically Distinct. Now with this information available, I went through the rest of the manuscript - some two hundred and ten pages - and in four other places I discovered the same phenomena I had associated with "language" B. Before I go on, the characteristics of "languages" A and B are obviously statistical. (I can't show you what they are here, as I don't have slides prepared. We can go into this matter in much greater detail in the discussions this afternoon.) Suffice it to say, the differences are obvious and statistically significant. There are two different series of agglomerations of symbols or letters, so that there are in fact two statistically distinguishable "languages."

Hands and "Languages" Elsewhere in the Manuscript. Now to go briefly through the manuscript: in the astrological section, there seemed to be no real differences that I could detect. The biological section* is all in one "language" (B) and one hand. The next section in which I noted a difference was the pharmaceutical section. Right in the middle of it, with ten folios on one side and ten on the other, there are six pages (two folios, folded so that there are three pages on each) which show a very obvious difference in hand: cramped, slanted, having quite a different character, very obvious even to the untrained eye. The frequency counts on this material bore out pretty much the same sort of findings that I had gotten in the herbal section. So we now have, in the pharmaceutical

*i.e., those folios featuring female figures. -Ed.

section, two "languages" and two hands. The recipe section at the end of the manuscript is somewhat of a mixture and didn't show the differences so neatly. It contains only one folio on which the writing differs noticeably to the eye from that on other folios; the statistical evidence gives some support to a "language" difference as well.

How Many Scribes Were There All Together? Summarizing, we have, in the herbal section, two "languages" which I call "Herbal A and B," and in the pharmaceutical section, two large samples, one in one "language" and one in the other, but in new and different hands. Now the fact of different "languages" and different hands should encourage us to go on and try to discover whether there were in fact only two different hands, or whether there may have been more. A closer examination of many sections of the manuscript revealed to me that there were not only two different hands; there were, in fact, only two "languages," but perhaps as many as eight or a dozen different identifiable hands. Some of these distinctions may be illusory, but in the majority of cases I feel that they are valid. Particularly in the pharmaceutical section, where the first ten folios are in a hand different from the middle six pages, I cannot say with any degree of confidence that the last ten pages are in fact in the same hand as the first ten.

Taken all together, it looks to me as if there were an absolute minimum of four different hands in the pharmaceutical section. I don't know whether they are different than those two which I previously mentioned as being in the herbal section, but they are certainly different from each other. So there are either four or six hands all together at this point. The final section of the manuscript contains only one folio which is obviously in a different hand than all the rest, and a count of the material in that one folio supports this; it is different, markedly different. I'm also positive it's different from anything I had seen before. So now we have a total of something like five or six to seven or eight different identifiable hands in the manuscript. This gives us a total of two "languages" and six to eight scribes (copyists, encipherers, call them what you will).

A New Slant on the Problem. These findings put an entirely different complexion on this problem than any that I think I have noted before in any other discussions or solutions. It's curious to me that a calligraphic or paleographic expert in one of the writings I have seen* says that the writing is consistent throughout, and is obviously the work of one man. Well, it obviously isn't, and I don't see how anyone who had any training could make any such statement, but there it is!

The Line Is a Functional Entity. In addition to my findings about "languages" and hands, there are two other points that I'd like to touch on very briefly. Neither of these has, I think, been discussed by anyone else before. The first point is that the line is a functional entity in the manuscript on all those pages where the text is presented linearly. There are three things about the lines that make me believe the line itself is a functional unit. The frequency counts of the beginnings and endings of lines are markedly

*"Some Impressions of the Voynich Manuscript," unpublished notes by Prof. A. H. Carter (Former technical historian, Army Security Agency), 1946, p. 1. -Ed.

different from the counts of the same characters internally. There are, for instance, some characters that may not occur initially in a line. There are others whose occurrence as the initial syllable of the first "word" of a line is about one hundredth of the expected. This, by the way, is based on large samples (the biggest sample is 15,000 "words"), so that I consider the sample to be big enough so that these statistics are significant.

The ends of lines contain what seem to be, in many cases, meaningless symbols: little groups of letters which don't occur anywhere else, and just look as if they were added to fill out the line to the margin. Although this isn't always true, it frequently happens. There is, for instance, one symbol that, while it does occur elsewhere, occurs at the end of the last "words" of lines 85% of the time. One more fact: I have three computer runs of the herbal material and of the biological material. In all of that, which is almost 25,000 "words," there is not one single case of a repeat going over the end of a line to the beginning of the next; not one. This is a large sample, too. These three findings have convinced me that the line is a functional entity, (what its function is, I don't know), and that the occurrence of certain symbols is governed by the position of a "word" in a line. For instance, there is a particular symbol which almost never occurs as the first letter of a "word" in a line except when it is followed by the letter that looks like "o."

Effect of "Word"-Final Symbols on the Initial Symbol of the Following "Word." The final point I will make concerns restrictions

I noticed, especially in the Biological section, on symbols that can end one "word" and symbols that begin the next "word." This occurs in other sections of the manuscript, especially in "language" B, but not as definitely as in "Biological B."*

<u>These Findings Should be Considered by Anyone Who Studies the Manuscript</u>. These findings are definite enough, I think, to warrant much further study by anyone who is going to be involved in seriously attacking the text of the Voynich manuscript. I have no interpretations of them, by the way; I have no solutions. All I know is that they are significant - and <u>damn</u> significant. Anyone who attempts to work on the text without considering these, ignores them at his own peril. They are <u>there</u>, and they are very definite. No matter which one of the forms that Mary originally mentioned** the material is considered to be, all of these other facts must be taken into consideration before anyone continues. The validity of text produced by any method at all must, I think, be judged against this statistical background.

That, I think, is all that I am prepared to say now, but this afternoon any of you who do come can review the points and ask me any questions you choose. I have a fairly large collection of statistical charts which will bear out most of the points that I have made. These have been reproduced, and with them my very brief notes on the four points I have made this morning.* Some of you now have copies of them. I think that the discussions this afternoon can be, indeed, quite fruitful if those of you who do have copies of my material would undertake to go through it and make up in your

*See Appendix A for details. -Ed.
**See pp. 7-8 above. -Ed.

own minds any questions or discussions that you'd like to go into this afternoon. Thanks very much.

II.A. Introduction to Afternoon Session. M. E. D'Imperio, Moderator.

Dr. Sydney Fairbanks will probably need no introduction for many, if not most, of those present, but for the sake of those few who may not know him, I will say a few words of introduction. After some early years in England, Dr. Fairbanks entered Harvard at the age of fifteen. He somehow managed to combine with his Harvard studies adventures as an ambulance driver in France, Italy, and Palestine during World War I, for which he was awarded the Croix de Guerre for courage under fire. He also served as an interpreter between French and Italian troops, and accompanied Ambassador Johnson to Rome as his private secretary.

Dr. Fairbanks next went to Harvard Law School and distinguished himself as a law student. He was an editor of the Harvard Law Review, and later practiced law with a Cleveland firm. He decided, however, that law was not the field for him in the long run; instead, he went back to Harvard and got a Doctorate in Middle English; he was elected to membership in the Frisian Academy in recognition of the excellence of his doctoral research. He then entered on a highly successful teaching career, culminating at St. Johns College in Annapolis.

At the outbreak of the Korean war, Dr. Fairbanks entered the cryptologic service and has performed many distinguished services to his country in that capacity. We are indeed privileged to have Dr. Fairbanks with us today to tell us of his research on the Voynich manuscript.

II.B. Suggestions Toward a Decipherment of the "Key." Dr. Sydney Fairbanks.

The research I am presenting today has been directed at the last three lines of the manuscript, on Folio 116 verso. Fig 3.a. shows these lines as they appear on the original.

The first line, omitting the final character, scans as a hexameter, which makes it sound impressive, but it is hardly informative. If the "-ton ola-" is omitted, it reads approximately "michi ... dabas multas de carcere portas," or "Thou gavest me ... many gates from prison." There are, however, so many inaccuracies and oddly-formed symbols that it seems reasonable to suppose that we are dealing with a cover message, with the anomalies dictated by the necessities of the covered message.

Looking at the first two lines, "abi" in the lower line, followed by "cere" in the upper, followed in turn by "a" in the lower, suggest a sort of "desultory rail-fence cipher," taking varying numbers of letters first from one line then from the other, but of course moving steadily from left to right. Since such a process is capable of producing many permutations, of which more than one may read intelligibly, the one I am about to select can only be defended if it is measurably superior to others, and critics are urged to present, using the same system, as many rival decipherments as possible.

Following this scheme, I found myself forced to the conclusion that the alternation started with the final 8 of "michiton oladaba8." The message, however, if I am correct, starts with or in the course of these two groups, though the system of encipherment must be different. One result of this scheme is to reduce the likelihood of noticing the rail fence.

We have then the arrangement shown in the next illustration (Fig 3.b.). Before making my rail-fence division, I shall make one or two adjustments, which must depend for justification on the results.

(1) The "mu" of "multχσ" starts, with apparent carelessness, with a short stroke above the preceding cross. (These crosses, by the way, seem designed only to mislead; as for carelessness, I believe that everything in these lines - even the smallest blot or stroke of the pen - is intentional and cannot be disregarded.) The result is that one can read equally well "imi" or "mu," and I shall choose the former.

(2) The s's written like 8's, and the obviously peculiar next-to-last symbol in "multχσ" I shall assume to be symbols standing, in the covered message, for letters other than the "s" and "o" they superficially resemble and stand for in the cover message.

(3) The third letter in "mo‹ix" I shall assume to be a "v" although the peculiar way in which it is formed - apparently a distortion of the symbol ⌐τ , must be designed to give some other information that I have not fathomed.

(4) The V that follows, occurring in "V‹x," looks, compared with the others, like a capital letter, and supports the assumption that "Vitare" begins a second sentence.

(5) The symbol " ‹ " in "v ‹ x" and "ab ‹ a" represents "ii."

(6) The "m" of "ma + ria" could equally well be "in," just as "mu" can be "imi."

(7) The first "e" in line 1 could equally well be "c."

(8) The final symbol "ɑ̃ " on the first line is an overlapping of ɑ and ŋ , "a" and "n."

Now, for our rail fence, we obtain the arrangement shown in the fourth illustration (Fig 3.d.). Since "removet" requires both a subject and an object, and "similem," being an accusative, modifies the object, I have extended (legitimately) my rail fence to the "8" of "oladaba8." The sentence may then read: "8 similem a t& removet e (or c). Vitare abiicere a in a, portat&r i a an." This may be translated: "C (or E) removes (i.e., distinguishes) the similarly-written 8 from the "tu" 8. To avoid casting off 'a' from 'in,' 'i' is carried by 'an'." The argument for "& " equal to "u" runs in three steps: (1) The first sentence says that unless "8" is removed it stands for "t& "; (2) the "8" of "porta8," having no "c" or "e" to remove it, stands for "t& "; (3) the only value for " & " that fits into "portat-r" is "u."

The digraph "ix," as we have seen, has to stand for "e" if the message is to be readable. The writer of the key gives the meanings of several symbols, but always indirectly, using a strange character resembling the cipher symbol in a position where it has to be replaced by the meaning of the symbol. In the case of "e" however he used a digraph that does not resemble a cipher symbol. Why? And he selects, though any digraph would serve, the only one that has the value of 9. Why? To my mind, the only adequate explanation is that he wishes to tell us - indirectly - that 9 = ix = e.

The way "tar" is written resembles very strongly the way the four symbols [symbol] , [symbol] , [symbol] , [symbol] are inserted as infixes in the symbol " rτ ," and I assume (as did the deviser of one of the alphabets for computer transcription I have seen) that "rτ " stands for "t." " ‹ ," I assume, represents " ‹ " and stands for "ii." I shall later give tentatively some evidence that ") " as part of a different character stands for "i," which raises a strong probability that " \ " also stands for "i." The statement that "To avoid casting off 'a' from 'in,' 'i' is carried by 'an'," must mean in cipher terms either that to avoid casting off " a\ " from " \\\," ") " is carried by "an," giving us " a " = "a," " \\ " = "n," " a\ " = " a) ," or that "c" = "a" and to avoid casting off "c" from " \\\ " or " \\\," ") " is carried by " a\ ." This looks as if " \ , \\ , and \\\ " were respectively equal to "i, n, and m." But we are still adrift as to the meaning and effect of "casting off." Similarly the first sentence does not tell us what 8 means when it has been "removed" by c or e.

This brings me to the third line of the key, which begins with a series of cipher symbols a‹o‹ rτa9 followed by the words "valscn ubren so nim gas mich o." Before I go further I want to draw a hard line between what I have said hitherto, presenting a method of decipherment, a reading of the first two lines, excluding the first two groups, and a series of derivable equivalents for \ ,) , ‹ , [symbol] , 9 , rτ , a\ , c ; these constitute, so to speak, my "thesis," and are supposed to hang together. What follows is a list of observations, made by me in endeavoring unsuccessfully to decipher "michiton oladaba." Some of them seem to me quite simple and probable, and others quite the reverse in both respects, but I am not asserting the consistency of any of them with the others. So, considering each one to be preceded with the word "perhaps," here they are.

1. Line 3 is concerned solely with "Michiton oladaba."

2. The cipher symbols may represent letters in these two groups.

3. ɑ< may represent the first two characters of line 1, and stand for "a (not cast off) ni."

4. ℴ< may stand for "on."

5. [illegible] / [illegible] may, consistently with the thesis, stand for "it."

6. The two c's may stand for two "i's," two "o's," or two "a's."

7. They may, consistently with the thesis, stand for two "a's."

8. " 9 " may, consistently with the thesis, stand for "e."

9. The final letter of "oladaba" may be an "e" cut short to make it look like "a" in the cover message.

10. If "michiton" is written above "oladaba" the result could be read (by rail fence) "o (a not cast off) nichil dat on ba."

11. "Nichil dat" may be more likely than "michi dabas, or dabat, or dat," since from the standpoint of information both "michi" and the second person singular are otiose.

12. Assuming "nichil dat," our unsolved message may have to

be formed from the pieces "o, a, a, nichil, dat, on, ba, e," which does not afford much scope.

13. On the analogy of "multo8" read "imiltu8" the apparent word "valsch" may be read "valscn."

14. The facts that in "michiton" and "mich" the "h" has a loop, that the "n" has no loop and that a convenient blot obscures the junction between "a," "c," and "n" may tend to confirm this.

15. ch may stand for "m."

16. The letters "mubren" can be transformed, by a regular process of moving each consonant clockwise into the place of the next, into the word "number," and this may be intentional.

17. The words "vals number" may mean "are in the wrong order."

18. If "o dat nichil," the final "o" of line 3 may be read "nichil."

19. The preceding word "mich" may be inserted to encourage the cover reading "michi," while the "o" conceals "nichil."

20. gAf , written so that it is almost "gaf," may be a compromise between "dabas" of the cover message and "dat" of the covered message.

This ends my list of possible but not necessarily probable building blocks.

I should say a few words in defense of the practicality of the "desultory rail-fence system." Anagrams, as Friedman pointed out, are not suitable for communication, and it may be objected that the rail-fence cipher suffers from the same defect of producing far too many choices to be practical. Further reflection on the matter will show, however, that the rail fence confronts us with a number of choices smaller by an order of magnitude: whereas an anagram of, e.g., seven letters provides 7!, or 5040 different choices, a rail-fence cipher of seven letters on two lines provides less than 2^7 or 128; I say "less than 128" because once all of one line has been used there is no choice about the remainder of the other line. To give you a chance to convince yourselves of this, I have provided you with two encipherments on one of the handouts (see Fig 4). The first is drawn from Bertrand Russell's History of Western Philosophy, and begins "He was somewhat..." It contains a proper name, "Hanover," and is, I hope, mildly amusing. The second encipherment is a part of a long sentence chosen at random from ten pages of Bacon's Opus Majus. It begins with the letters "ae," and breaks off in the middle of a list of words. It is not amusing. My intention is to demonstrate that different people will independently get the same result from deciphering them.

I hope these remarks will be of some use to you. My reason, as you might surmise, for not keeping them to myself is that I hope someone will get the answer while I am still around to read it. It might even be one of us!

(Editorial Note: The above is a written version of his presentation which was kindly provided to me by Dr. Fairbanks for inclusion in these proceedings.)

3.a. "Key" Sentences, Folio 116v (Photocopy)

3b.

MICHITON OLADABAS MULTρδ + TE + TAR CERE + PORTAδ + m

SIX + MARIX + MOVIX + VIX + AB<A + MA + RIA +

① MU = IMI ③ ∨ = V ⑥ < = II

② ρ AND δ ≠ O AND S ④ Capital V ⑥ M = IN

3c.

δ IMILTρ δ TETARCERE PORTAδ m

SIXMARIXMOVIXVIIXABIIA INARIA

⑦ E or C ⑧ m = an ⑨ ρ = u

⑩ δ = TU ⑪ IX = E

3d.

δ (IMIL)(TU δ)(TE)(TAR)(CERE)(PORTATU)(m)

S)(EMA)(REMOVE)(VI)(EABII)(A IN A)(RI A)

3e.

δ SIMILEM A TU δ REMOVET E[C].

VITARE ABIICERE A IN A, PORTATUR I A m.

Fig. 3. Steps in Analyzing the Voynich Key

(Dr. Fairbanks)

HEW MEW ME NA NEW KGLAY HE TO NORRIE
ASSO HATA BOU TMOY HENA YOU DO FTCO

DHEDTO VER THELE WEDI PRENTCO STIFU
URFHA VERMA USEGI HEWHA CALDA DNGSENSI

FULMA NDI NTHE DVINO GIVW NG[illegible]OW HACU RE
NGOSE XIMSE GWITHA CETTO EUPASHI THA

SBANDHI DENTRE COTHE RHE DESW ETEFU
TSHEDSE DAHU STORY OSO RDWHE TBRI REGRAL

ASTMMSGITINUNTMLIAIDCTOIBUECMPOAEPAASS
EIAUIURLGAMOSRATNSIINSESSOSITMTUCEEVA

CCUALUMLNURUUMMNACUNIERMUSTELNUAIEIUM
BLAIARIGAMCTAEQUECMMTUTIRINDIGISLNSTD

USSYHSERCSAUSBOUSAASEOPTEAT....
OCPUCLIULICDIALSTHNAGARMER......

Fig. 4. Encipherments (Dr. Fairbanks)

II.C. The Solution Claim of Dr. Robert S. Brumbaugh. M. E. D'Imperio.

I feel that, for the sake of completeness, this seminar should include a brief summary of another recent decipherment claim. Robert S. Brumbaugh, a professor of medieval philosophy at Yale University, became interested in the Voynich manuscript during the thirties. When it was donated to Yale in 1969, he began to attack it in earnest. He was also struck by botanist Hugh O'Neill's identification of American plants in the drawings. Brumbaugh published an article in the journal Speculum in 1974, announcing that he had solved the mystery. In 1975, he published a second article in the Yale University Library Gazette giving some further details. He claims to have read some labels on plant pictures and some other words on various pages of the manuscript. He also states that he has deciphered the name of Roger Bacon in the "key" sentences on the last page. He regards the manuscript as a deliberate forgery for the purpose of fooling Emperor Rudolph the Second of Bohemia into parting with the large sum of money he paid for it.

Brumbaugh makes considerable use of the "key"-like sentences others have noted on folios 1 recto, 17 recto, 49 verso, 66 recto, 57 verso and 116 verso. He says that these sequences were primarily intended to mislead the would-be decipherer, but they still provided aid to him, Brumbaugh, in penetrating the cipher, because the forger outsmarted himself and gave too much away. His explanations of these clues are, unfortunately, very incomplete. They are convincing at first glance, but when I tried to look more closely at them and retrace the steps Brumbaugh claimed to have followed, they fell apart. To make matters worse, Brumbaugh offers no documentation or scholarly evidence of his sources other than a few off-hand, very vague words in passing.

For example, consider the sentences on folio 116 verso, which Dr. Fairbanks has studied so carefully from an entirely different point of view. Brumbaugh finds some phrases there to be enciphered in what he calls a "standard thirteenth-century cipher." He offers no evidence in the literature of just which cipher he means. He claims to find confirmation for his idea about this standard cipher in the paired alphabetical sequences which are very faintly and fragmentarily visible in the right and left margins of folio 1 recto. These are not visible at all in our photocopy, but may be seen in Father Petersen's remarkable hand transcript, a photocopy of which is here for anyone to examine during our break periods. Brumbaugh claims to find in these sequences a monoalphabetic substitution of two normal alphabets, with "a" of one set against "d" of the other. I can see no evidence that the alphabets are offset at all in Petersen's transcript, which was carefully matched and corrected by him against the original.

But using this cipher and some rearrangement of other syllables, Brumbaugh obtains the name RODG BACON from the phrases he singles out on folio 116 verso. This is the planted reference to Bacon that he claims was intended to attract Rudolph's cipher experts into advising the Emperor to buy the manuscript.

On folio 66 recto, Brumbaugh sees a set of "formulae" in the words and letters scattered down the right margin. These formulae, he claims, serve to equate symbols to other symbols in the Voynich script by a sort of "cryptarithmetic." He gives some examples of this in his 1975 paper. The only evidence he gives for his idea is the following rather airy sentence: "Since I had seen a number of these characters in another cipher in Milan, where they represented numerals, I suspected an arithmetical game." He provides no further support or explanation of his sources. Unfortunately, as I soon discovered while researching my monograph on the Voynich manuscript, there are literally hundreds, perhaps thousands, of early Italian ciphers which use numeral forms as cipher characters, many of them very similar to some Voynich script characters. None of these ciphers, however, seem to include any such cryptarithmetic as Brumbaugh claims to see on folio 66 recto. Without a better reference, we cannot track down the source upon which he bases his idea. While I will admit that the small number of formulae he explains in full are plausible enough as they stand, I have been unable to extend the same principles to all the other examples on that page which he does not explain, and in fact some actually seem to contradict the method he suggests.

Using these "equations" and some recoveries of labels for plants, Brumbaugh set up a nine-by-four matrix. The plant labels, all on folio 100 recto, he got by cribbing and by using word patterns with repeated letters like the p and e in "pepper," and guesses at what plants the pictures showed. Again, Brumbaugh claims that the nine-by-four matrix is similar to "a standard alchemist's or astrologer's cipher, well known in the trade," and as usual, he provides no further reference or explanation to back up this claim.

All the Voynich symbols, according to Brumbaugh's theory, stand for forms of the numerals one through nine. The encipherment is a two-step operation. First, letters of plaintext are replaced by numerals using the nine-by-four box, collapsing the letters of the alphabet onto the nine numerals. This slide (Fig 5.) shows the matrix as Brumbaugh published it in his paper. For instance, the letters B, K, and R were all replaced by the number 2. Then, as a second step, a choice was made among several different fanciful designs for each numeral to conceal them, producing the Voynich cipher text as we see it. According to Brumbaugh, the symbols were chosen from "modern and archaic numeral forms, Greek and Latin letters, and several cursive compendia." Again, he gives no evidence or detailed explanation of the origin of any particular symbol, so we have nothing to go on.

The next slide shows a matrix with some of the Voynich symbol variants for numeral forms (Fig 6.). This is my own tentative reconstruction of the cipher correspondence from Brumbaugh's articles, since he does not explicitly provide them anywhere. We see here, for example, that there are four Voynich symbols all standing for the numeral 7. There are some uncertainties, for reasons to be discussed in a moment.

Decipherment involves three steps; first, recognizing the numbers underlying the multiple variants in the Voynich script. Second, writing, under each numeral the two, three, or four possible choices for plaintext equivalents. Third, selecting a pronounceable and plausible Latin-like word out of the resulting rows of letters. The plaintext produced is described by Brumbaugh himself as follows: "An artificial language, based on Latin, but not very firmly based there; its spelling is phonetically impressionistic; some sample passages seem solely repetitive padding." Also, the "upper cipher key" (whatever that may be) changes slightly every eight pages.

This slide (Fig 7.) shows two of Brumbaugh's sample decipherments to illustrate his method, and some of the problems I encountered in reconstructing it. The top example is from folio 116 verso. He reads this as ARABYCCUS, supposedly referring to the Arabic numerals of the cipher. Even granting his identification of the Voynich characters and his matrix, it could as easily be read ARAKYLLUS, ABARYLLUS, UBARYCCI, or any number of other more or less pronounceable, Latin-like things.

The bottom one is from folio 100 recto. This is a page containing rows of small plant pictures each labelled with a Voynich script sequence. Brumbaugh reads this as a garbled word for PAPAVERUS or "poppy." But then he seems to have gotten in a hurry or mixed up in his interpretation of the Voynich characters; he apparently sees the fourth letter as an O-like symbol, corresponding to the numeral 1 and plaintext A, whereas I see it clearly as an A-like symbol. I cannot account at all for his interpretation of the fifth letter as a plaintext V. In almost all of his other sample decipherments, there is at least one such letter that is puzzling, or can be interpreted differently from his choice. There is a "messiness" about the whole affair that is not satisfying. Attempts to extend the recoveries to labels on other pages result in many meaningless sequences that bear no relation to Latin or anything else, with one or two slightly more promising instances now and then, to keep us "hooked" and keep us trying.

A new paper by Brumbaugh is scheduled to appear in the 1976 issue of the Journal of the Warburg and Courtauld Institutes of the University of London, probably to be published in early 1977. We can hope that he will provide a more carefully worked-out and documented exposition of his theory there so that we may subject it to independent verification.

INTERMEDIATE CIPHER

PLAIN	1	2	3	4	5	6	7	8	9
	A	B	C	D	E	F	G	H	I
	J	K	L	M	N	O	P	Q	
		R		S		T		U	US
	V		W	(X)	X		Y		Z

Fig. 5. Brumbaugh's Matrix

CIPHER	[illegible]? O	[illegible]	[illegible]	[illegible]	a	[illegible]	[illegible]	8	9
	1	2	3	4	5	6	7	8	9
PLAIN	A	B	C	D	E	F	G	H	I
	J	K	L	M	N	O	P	Q	
		R		S		T		U	US
	V		W	(X)	X		Y		Z

Fig. 6. Reconstructed Cipher Correspondences

Folio 116v

0	2	0	2	7	3	3	9
A	B	A	B	G	C	C	I
J	K	J	K	P	L	L	
Y	R	Y	R	Y	W	W	-US

"ARABYCCUS"

Folio 100r

7	1	7	5	2	1	7	1	4
G	A	G	E	B	A	G	A	D
P	J	P	N	K	J	P	J	M
Y	V	Y	X	R	V	Y	V	S
			?	?				

"PAPAVAYJS"
ER

Fig. 7. Two Sample Decipherments by Brumbaugh

II.D. <u>Further Details of New Statistical Findings</u>. Capt. Prescott Currier.

1. <u>The Nature of the Symbols</u>. I've looked at most of these letters under a magnifying glass, so I think I know how they were all actually made. These letters: o, 8, 9, 2 all seem to start with a "c"-curve, which was made first, in this direction: ⟲c , so we have: o = c + ɔ, 8 = c + ℓ, 9 = c + ɔ, 2 = c + ɔ. These forms all have counterparts starting with ι : 8 = ι8, 9 = ι9, 2 = ι2 , etc. we also have a = c + \ . All the letters containing an initial "c"-curve are also the only letters that can be preceded in the same word by the little letter that looks like "c," e.g., c89, ccc89 . On the other hand, the letters R and 2 (which have very high frequencies) can <u>never</u> be preceded by c , <u>ever</u>; they are instead preceded by a .

The final letters (that is, the ones that I call finals, although they can also occur elsewhere) are in two series, one preceded by a and the other by o , giving a series of sixteen:

ɔ	iɔ	iiɔ	iiiɔ
R	(iR)	(iiR)	(iiiR)
2	i2	(ii2)	(iii2)
rf	irf	(iirf)	(iiirf)

The ones in parentheses are very low-frequency; the others all occur with respectable frequency. In addition, these combinations of symbols which appear as finals may occur separately - "unattached finals," as I call them. A large number of unattached finals is a characteristic of "Language" B, and <u>not</u> "Language" A, by the way.

All of this indicates to me that considerable thought was put into how this mess was made up. We have the fact that you can make up almost any of the other letters out of these two symbols ι and c ; it doesn't <u>mean</u> anything, but it's interesting.

2. <u>Origin of the Symbols</u>. This symbol 9 is a common Latin abbreviation standing for CON, CUM or -US, so that it can come at both the beginnings and ends of words. For example, "continuus" might be written "9tinu9." Now 9 is one of the few symbols in the manuscript that does in fact occur at beginnings and endings of frequent words, especially in combination with the , series. It looks as if whoever designed the alphabet used 9 because this symbol resembled the one used throughout medieval Latin for CON, -US, a frequent initial and final. I think that's the source of that particular letter.

As for σ , it is a frequent letter in Etruscan, in Lydian, and in the Lemnos alphabet, but there that letter always had the value "F," never "S." In medieval Latin on occasion it did represent "S." This symbol could have been taken from these other alphabets.

You can pick out resemblances between Latin abbreviations and other alphabets for most symbols except for the series , , , . The symbol looks very much like a medieval Latin abbreviation for "tinus." The last two look as if they are simply variations of the first two, with the second vertical stroke pushed back. They (,) appear 90-95% of the time in the first lines of paragraphs, in some 400 occurrences in one section of the manuscript.

One might conclude that , are an elaborate form of , , with the same value. This is often the case in medieval manuscripts, especially in illuminated ones; certain letters have magnified, aberrant, beautified forms. But, not true! These two letters , are not the same as those two , , as the statistics show. The letters , are followed anywhere in a "word" by our little friend about half the time (say 750 out of a total of 1500), including initially. These two, , , are never, ever, anywhere in the manuscript, followed by . These latter symbols are much less frequent than the first two, but their occurrence followed by is zero. I don't have to calculate sigmages on that! Therefore, , are not aberrant or variant forms of , , but separate letters in their own right. This holds true through the whole manuscript. That is one of the peculiar things about the manuscript: we have two "languages" - they are definite, no doubt about it at all - but there are features like this that follow through from one "language" to another. That's just an item of incidental intelligence; there it is, for what it's worth.

Question (D'Imperio): I wonder about the cases where the two loops of and are separated from each other, and one end comes down in the middle of another word, often on top of that little letter like a table, ?

Currier: That may be a way of abbreviating two of those looped letters. It doesn't happen frequently enough to bother me.

(Example: [symbols])

3. <u>Different Frequencies of Symbols at Beginnings, Middles, and Ends of Lines</u>. At beginnings and ends of lines, we have skewed frequencies. For example, let's take these two letters [symbol] and [symbol] . (This letter [symbol] , by the way, is in fact made like this: [symbol] .) Here are statistics from "Herbal A" material, about 6500 words, 1000 lines, averaging seven words per line:

"word"-initial symbols	total frequency as "word"-initial	expected in any "word"	actual, in first "word"
[symbol]	118	20	3
[symbol]	212	38	26
[symbol]	24	4,5	0
[symbol]	45	10	10

If its occurrence as an initial were random, we would expect it to occur one seventh of the time in each word position of a line. Actually, it is a very infrequent word initial at the beginning of a line, except when there is an intercalated o . This applies only to "Language" A, by the way; words with this initial group are low in "Language" B ([symbol] , for example, occurs only 5 times in Herbal B, but 212 times in Herbal A).

4. <u>The Nature of the Symbols [symbol] , [symbol] , [symbol] , [symbol] .</u> My next point concerns the so-called "ligatures" based, apparently, on the series [symbol] , [symbol] , [symbol] , [symbol] . They are made like this, by the way: [symbol] , with [symbol] , etc., written on top of it. In Herbal A material, in fact in all A material, this series is initially high; in B, it is very low - another way

of identifying the two "languages." In Herbal A, the word-initial occurrences are as follows:

symbol	all "word" initials	first "word" of line
	326	3
	67	1
	82	0
	14	0

These "ligatures" seem to behave almost, but not quite, like , . In contrast, whether or not followed by , , , or , the series , , , are very high in both "languages," and frequently as paragraph and line initials. The "ligatures" can never occur as paragraph initial, and almost never line initial.

Therefore, , , and the like are symbols in their own right, and are not equal to or , etc. These statistical considerations are the reason why I made up my alphabet the way I did; I restricted it as much as possible to letters in their own right, not ligatures.

5. Effects of the Ending of One "Word" on the Beginning of the Next "Word." You remember I mentioned that some "word"-finals have an obvious and statistically-significant effect on the initial symbol of a following "word." This is almost exclusively to be found in "Language" B, and especially in "Biological B" material.

For example, we have:

"words" ending in:	Next "word" begins with:		
	4o	8 or 2	cc or cc
8 series	13	7	91
2 series	10	2	68
ɔ series	23	0	275
9 series	592	184	168

(The above figures are condensed from Table 5A, Appendix A.)

"Words" ending in the 9 sort of symbol, which is very frequent, are followed about four times as often by "words" beginning with 4o . That is a fact, and it holds true throughout the entire twenty pages of "Biological B." It's something that has to be considered by anyone who does any work on the manuscript. These phenomena are <u>consistent</u>, <u>statistically significant</u>, and hold true throughout those areas of text where they are found. I can think of no linguistic explanation for this sort of phenomenon, not if we are dealing with words or phrases, or the syntax of a language where suffixes are present. In no language I know of does the suffix of a word have anything to do with the beginning of the next word.

- - - - - - - - - - -

(At this point, Captain Currier's presentation was concluded, and questions were raised by listeners. The lengthy and interesting discussion that followed, transcribed in its entirety from our tape record, comprises the next section of these notes. -Ed.)

II.E. Questions and Discussion.

Question (Speaker not identified): How do you account for the full-word repeats?

Currier: That's just the point - they're not words!

Child: I don't think you can say that doesn't happen. Now, it may not happen with the languages in a more or less consistent, normative writing system. But it does when a scribe is noting rapid speech, with all its slurs and elisions, rather than the facts of grammar. The sounds at the end of one word can influence those at the beginning of the next.

Currier: Not this much.

D'Imperio: Could I suggest that it may be related to the constraints on groups in a system like a code or synthetic language, when words from certain pages or parts of the code combine preferentially with words from certain other parts of the code?

Currier: Precisely, precisely; yes, right.

Valaki: What about sounds at the beginning of one word being changed by neighboring sounds, at the end of the previous word? This happens in some languages (examples from Greek which are not audible on the tape. -Ed.)

Currier: I don't think it would happen to this extent...Has anyone seen my computer run on "Biological B?"

<u>D'Imperio</u>: I haven't seen that - I'd certainly like to get a copy!

<u>Currier</u>: "Biological B" is by far the most interesting; <u>very constrained</u>, very interesting from a statistical point of view. (Some examples, not clear on the tape -Ed.) I have a whole notebook of statistical charts at home: things I wanted to look into, and took various samples of limited areas of text. But I think anyone who's really interested ought to do their own. These are the best kind of evidence for valid conclusions. If you want to make an assumption of a value for some particular symbol, with an index you can try it out and see what happens. Certain things will also arise from taking these statistics which will provide evidence for a new theory. If you view all these statistics as basic background evidence on which to base theories, you can come up with a hypothesis which can be tested, rather than <u>starting</u> with a hypothesis and then looking for evidence to back it up. This statistical background is the sort of evidence anyone who is going to work on this document should be aware of. It gives you something against which you can compare the material and test your hypotheses.

<u>Question</u> (Speaker unidentified): Have there been any studies on the lengths of words?

<u>Currier</u>: Not specifically. I've got it all at home...but it hasn't suggested anything to me.

<u>D'Imperio</u>: I made a partial study of word lengths on a small scale (15,000 characters); few words were longer than seven or eight symbols

or shorter than two.

<u>Currier</u>: But there <u>are</u> a lot that are exactly two long. (Examples from "Herbal A" and "Herbal B," not audible on tape -Ed.) Certain groups - a different one in A than in B material - are repeated four times in a row; they would <u>have</u> to be numbers, I can't think of anything else. If the one were "zero" in "Herbal A," the other might be the "zero" in "Herbal B," and this would be what you'd look up in your artificial language system. I don't believe that, by the way.

This statistical data of mine is available - my notes and observations. I've come to no real conclusions, except that this can't be, as far as I can see, a straightforward simple encipherment of any linguistic data; there has to be an intermediate step somewhere as far as I can see.

<u>Question</u> (Speaker unidentified): You said that each line was a separate sentence unto itself...

<u>Currier</u>: An annoying little circumstance: words beginning with " cꞇ " almost never seem to occur first in a line. I thought perhaps I might try numerals one to ten for the letters that come before " cꞇ " in line-initial position, but I can't make it work. But this kind of thing makes it look as if the line is a functional entity; that is what bothers me. I can't interpret the data!

<u>Question</u> (Speaker unidentified): Is that true all the way through the manuscript?

Currier: Yes, it is basically true, but especially in "Biological B."

D'Imperio: There seem to be very strong constraints in combinations of symbols; only a very limited number of letters occur with each other letter in certain positions of a "word."

Currier: Yes...(Examples, not clear on tape. -Ed.) By the way, if anyone does transcribe any more text, I wish they would use my alphabet; then we can put all the data and results together.

D'Imperio: I have a copy of Captain Currier's alphabet and sorting sequence.

Currier: You don't need to bother about the sorting sequence. I had a particular reason for it back when I did the earlier work but you don't need it now. I'd like to see someone do more with the problem, in the "Recipe" section for example. You should be careful when you transcribe, though; you have to make some judgements of what a letter is, and it takes practice to get the hang of it.

Miller: I'd like to bring up something relating to Mary's introduction this morning, where she associated my name with the theory that the manuscript was meaningless. I would object to the phrase "meaningless doodles," because I think this is purposeful but inarticulate writing; doodles are simply to pass the time away...

D'Imperio: But the point I was emphasizing was that this theory considered the manuscript meaningless within our context of trying to decipher it...

Miller: The meaning is irrecoverable. If there is such a school of thought, [of people who believe that the meaning of the manuscript is inherently and essentially irrecoverable -Ed.], who else is in it besides me?

D'Imperio: There are some people who come pretty close: Dr. MacClintock, for example, thinks it's almost entirely irrecoverable, I believe...

Miller: Has this been argued on the basis of a careful analysis of the text, or merely because it isn't readable? I don't think the thing is a hoax. But no details have been given of the theories (that the meaning is irrecoverable) and I would like to read more about it.

D'Imperio: I think it's primarily exasperation on the part of people that have been frustrated time and again in attempting to decipher it, and they just end up saying "Oh, fooey! How can the thing mean anything, with all these weird repeats and such...?"

Miller: But with all these statistics that Captain Currier, Brigadier Tiltman, and Mr. Friedman have given - hasn't anyone...

D'Imperio: The trouble is, how can you prove that something is meaningless, or that its meaning is irrecoverable? That is just what is left after you've disproven all the specific positive decipherment theories you or anyone else has thought of so far. But another good one might still always come along. (Editorial comment: If we were to prove scientifically that a text's meaning is irrecoverable, we would require either (1) a theory that provided for certain observable criteria or characteristics that strings having recoverable meanings must have, and a proof that this particular text does not exhibit those criteria; or (2) a theory providing for certain observable criteria which strings having irrecoverable meanings must have, and a proof that this particular string before us does exhibit those criteria. This would constitute a sort of "uncomputability" or "undecidability" theory for the semantics of textual strings. Is this possible? At our present stage of knowledge, I sincerely doubt it. Still, it raises some highly interesting philosophical questions that deserve further attention from someone qualified to explore them. There are, of course, tests for "psychological random" characteristics of various sorts, which would provide some strong support for a hypothesis that the text had been fabricated, independently of any semantic or linguistic structure having a recoverable meaning; these tests and hypotheses ought certainly to be applied to the Voynich text.)

Valaki: Some time ago I saw a screen for sale at a furniture store. It was a four-panel screen; on one panel there was writing in Greek, which I read and found to be one of Aesop's fables. When I tried to read the second panel, I couldn't make any sense out of it - nothing went with anything else. I finally realized that they were just individual Greek words copied off at random. The third panel was just Greek letters, and the fourth panel was imitation Greek letters!

D'Imperio: I wish you had bought it - what a beautiful test case! We could have made some frequency counts on it and...

Valaki: Maybe that's like the Voynich - it could turn out to be a good straight copying job.

D'Imperio: But still, back to Doris' point, how can we demonstrate that? You see, the way you realized that about the screen - the fact that the other panels were meaningless - was because you knew Greek and you read the fable on the first panel. Then, when you looked at the others, you saw the degradation...

Valaki: I really thought my Greek had gone! Nothing was matching anything else; words didn't go together. I sort of went backwards to attack it.

D'Imperio: Well, with the Voynich, we are in the position of having something we can't read any part of, to any degree, and that doesn't look like anything we've ever seen before. How can we show, demonstrate, that it is meaningless?

Miller: You don't have to demonstrate....

Currier: Nobody has tried, not that I know of.

D'Imperio: No, not that I've ever seen.

Currier: Evidence that it can't be "doodles" is the minimum of six people involved in the production. I can prove four beyond a shadow of a doubt. I'm not a paleographer; I wouldn't stand up in court and try to defend this against a paleographer. But I'm positive, particularly in the Herbal Section. I imagine it to have happened something like this: some sixty-five folios were prepared ahead of time with drawings on them. They were placed on a table so. The first twenty-five folios were taken, one at a time, off the top and filled in with writing by one individual. At the end of those twenty-five, he got very tired and he called for help. Another man sat down opposite him at the same table. And they took them off, one at a time: one man took one off and did his thing, in his own "language," while the other man did his thing with another in his "language." And they went through the second stack and interleaved them; one man did it one way and the other man did it the other way. When they were done, they had the Herbal Section!

Question (Speaker unidentified): Are you convinced that the page numbering is correct?

Currier: Yes. I am sure the page numbering is that of the original...

Question (Speaker unidentified): What about the fact that there were no erasures? That makes it look like a copying job.

Currier: It must be a copying job. But how do two people copying from a single source produce material in two different "languages" simultaneously? I can just see them sitting there! I'm absolutely positive this is the way it was done. The folios were prepared in advance by someone else with the drawings on them. Sometimes the writing overlaps the drawings somewhat. The pictures of the Herbal Section look as if they were drawn by a single individual, but this I couldn't prove. The writing on folios 1 to 25 was done by one man.

On folios 26 to 65, it was done by two men, one who worked a little faster (the man who did the first batch did more of the second batch; he was more experienced).

Buck: It was noted that some pages are missing, and the cover is missing. Do you have any ideas about the reason?

Currier: No, I have no theories.

Miller: Somebody stripped off the beautiful pictures!

Currier: Then he left a lot of beautiful pictures behind!

D'Imperio: One of the missing folios was for the zodiac signs of Capricorn and Aquarius; maybe that was somebody's horoscope?

Question (Speaker unidentified): When a new hand takes over, do you see variations in the mode of writing the symbols?

Currier: Yes, but it's the overall impression of the writing. In general, for example, in "Herbal A," the writing is upright, rounded, lines are well-spaced, it looks clean, clear, with no extraneous material. "Herbal B," in contrast, is uphill, slanted cramped writing. It's obvious to me. The first thing I noted looking at the manuscript as a whole was this difference in the writing in the Herbal Section, before I had taken a single count. I separated the pages by sight first, then took a ten-page sample in each of the two separate writings, and made separate counts. It stared me in the face - there it was: all my selections were correct. It was a sufficiently controlled procedure to make me think these conclusions are valid. Anyone can see it - just lay the pages out and look. I can't prove the pages are in the right order, but I just <u>feel</u> that they are. In the Astrological Section, the signs of the zodiac are in the right order.

<u>D'Imperio</u>: There is some evidence in the folio gatherings - the numbers in the bottom corners of some pages, about every eight folios. They agree well with the folio numbering at the beginning of the manuscript, at least. They also show some relatively early forms of the numerals. This gives us a bit more evidence that some of the pages at least are in the right order.

<u>Buck</u>: I would like to speculate about where the missing pages are...

<u>D'Imperio</u>: Maybe they'll show up some day, among somebody's papers!

- - - - - - - - - - - - - -

APPENDIX A

The VOYNICH MANUSCRIPT
Some notes and observations

Capt. P. H. Currier

October 1976

1. The matter of 'hands'

It was noted early in the study of the Herbal Section (pp 1-112) that the handwriting characteristics of several pairs of adjacent folios varied perceptibly, even to an untrained eye. A few elementary frequency counts showed that the statistical profiles of the textual material on these folios also differed significantly. Further investigation of all the folios in the section revealed that there were two different 'hands' in use throughout the entire section, each writing in its own 'language,' hereinafter called Languages A and B.

With this evidence at hand a check of the remaining sections of the Manuscript turned up the following:

(a) In the Astrological Section (pp 113-146) there seemed to be no significant difference in the writing on any of the folios except that there appeared to be a 'foreign' element evident in the inclusion of a few symbols which occur nowhere else in the Manuscript. The 'language' throughout is mostly A but without some of the more pronounced 'A' features found in Herbal A.

(b) The Biological Section (pp 147-166) appears to be the work of a single scribe, all in Language 'B,' with strong, sharply delineated statistical characteristics. The language of this section is more restricted, perhaps even more 'regular' than the language 'B' in other sections of the Manuscript. This could conceivably be the result of this section being the product of only one person.

(c) In the <u>Pharmaceutical Section</u> (pp 167-211), pp 167-173 and two folios (pp 193-198) in the mid-portion of the section are in Language 'B'; the remaining folios are in Language 'A.' An interesting point here is the fact that there seemed to be more than the expected two 'hands,' one for each 'language' as in the Herbal Section. The difference between the 'B' writing of the mid-portion (pp 193-198) and the 'A' writing of the surrounding folios (pp 179-192; pp 199-211) is obvious and easily discernible and was noted on the first quick pass through the Manuscript. But it is not at all clear that the initial Language 'B'-folios (pp 167-173) are in the same hand as pp 193-198 nor can it be said with certainty that the Language 'A'-folios (pp 179-192 and pp 199-211) are all the work of a single individual. Additionally, p 174 is in Language 'A" and in a hand different from any other in the Pharmaceutical Section.

The Newbold foliation indicates that the Biological Section extends through ff 85-86 and it would appear from the illustrations that the Pharmaceutical Section does not begin until f 87. However, frequency counts before and after the break at f 84/f 85 indicate a change from Biological material to something else. For example, the final ' o89 ,' which does not occur in the Biol. B text, shows up in ff 85-86 with quite a respectable frequency and matches the frequency of this final in the Pharmaceutical 'B' text on ff 94-95. I am reasonably certain that the handwriting on ff 85-86 is not the same as that on ff 95-96 but I cannot be sure that it differs from the Biol. B hand. In sum, I would venture a guess that there are at least three and perhaps as many as five or six different hands in evidence in this section. On the other 'hand' it may all be an illusion.

(d) The Recipe Section (pp 212-234) contains only one folio on which the writing differs noticeably from that on the other folios. This difference is supported to a degree by statistical evidence. The 'language' throughout the Section is 'modified B' (i.e., contains certain 'A' characteristics). It might be worth noting, however, that there seem to be some less discernible handwriting variations on many other folios in the Recipe Section. I cannot be sure that these are valid differences but the frequency counts of the material on the folios in question are just slightly supportive.

2. The matter of 'language'

It should be noted before going on that the word 'language' is quite loosely used here and throughout these notes. It connotes only a marked statistical difference between two sets of text. It in no way implies the existence of any underlying language. Being convenient however, it will continue to be used.

As previously stated in para. 1 above, the Herbal Section contains both Language 'A' and 'B.' The principle differences between the two 'languages' in this Section are:

(a) Final ' 89 ' is very high in Language 'B'; almost non-existent in Language 'A.'

(b) The symbol groups ' [illegible] ' and ' [illegible] ' are very high in 'A' and often occur repeated; low in 'B.'

(c) The symbol groups ' [illegible] ' and ' [illegible] ' rarely occur in 'B'; medium frequency in 'A.'

(d) Initial ' [illegible] ' high in 'A'; rare in 'B.'

(e) Initial ' [illegible] ' very high in 'A'; very low in 'B.'

(f) 'Unattached' finals scattered throughout Language 'B' texts in considerable profusion; generally <u>much</u> less noticeable in Language 'A.'

These features are to be found generally in the other Sections of the manuscript although there are always local variations; which of course could imply a 'subject-matter' effect.

The discovery of the two 'languages' in the Herbal Section was the principle reason for transcribing and indexing this material. It was hoped that by the application of comparative techniques to the Herbal A and B texts, ostensibly dealing with identical subject matter, some clue to the nature of the two 'systems of writing' might be forthcoming. The results were completely negative; there was no sign of parallel constructions or any other evidence that was useful in this regard. It was impossible not to conclude that (a) we were not dealing with a 'linguistic' recording of data and (b) the illustrations had little to do with the accompanying text. Study of other sections of the Manuscript where 'A' and 'B' texts are found has produced nothing to alter this conclusion. Further, it has so far proved impossible to categorize or to classify grammatically any series of 'words' or to discern any use patterns that would suggest any recognizable syntactic arrangement of the underlying text. Perhaps even more important, I have been unable to identify 'words' or individual symbols in either 'language' to which I could assign even tentative numerical values. It seems quite incredible to me that any systems of writing (or a simple substitution thereof) would not betray one or both of the above features.

3. <u>The effect of word-final symbols on the initial symbol of the following 'word'</u>

This 'word-final effect' first became evident in a study of the Biol. B index wherein it was noted that the final symbol of 'words' preceding 'words' with an initial ' 4o ' was restricted pretty largely to ' 9 '; and that initial 'cτ /c²τ' was preceded much more frequently than expected by finals of the ' iiD '-series and the ' 8 '-series. Additionally, 'words' with initial ' cτ /c²τ ' occur in line-initial position far <u>less</u> frequently than expected, which perhaps might be construed as being preceded by an 'initial nil.'

This phenomenon occurs in other sections of the Manuscript, especially in those 'written' in Language B, but in no case with quite the same definity as in Biological B. Language A texts are fairly close to expected in this respect.

I can think of no interpretation of this phenomenon, linguistic or otherwise. Inflexional endings would certainly not have this effect nor would any other grammatical feature that I know of if we assume that we are dealing with <u>words</u>. If, however, these word-appearing elements are something else, syllables, letters, even digits, restrictions of this sort might well occur.

4. The line as a functional entity

As mentioned in para. 3. above, 'words' with initial ' [Voynich] / [Voynich] ' are unexpectedly low in line initial position (on average about .1 of expected); other 'words' occur in this position far more frequently than expected, particularly 'words' with initial ' [Voynich],' ' [Voynich],' etc., which have the appearance of ' [Voynich] '-initial 'words' suitably modified for line-initial use. Symbol groups at the ends of lines are frequently of a character unlike those appearing in the body of the text sometimes having the appearance of fillers. Further, in only one instance so far noted has a repeated sequence (of 'words') extended beyond the end of one line into the beginning of the next.

All in all it is difficult not to assume that the line, on those pages on which the text has a linear arrangement, is a self-contained unit with a function yet to be discovered.

5. Appended Tables

Table A. Voynich Manuscript foliation-pagination concordance with an indication of 'language' and 'hand' where known.

Table 1. Frequency of initials with medial ' [Voynich] ' and ' [Voynich] ' for all sections showing both total and line-initial frequencies.

Table 2. Frequency of finals following ' [Voynich] / [Voynich] ' for all sections of the Manuscript.

Table 3. Frequency of finals following medial ' [Voynich] ' and ' [Voynich] ' for Herb. A, Herb. B and Biol. B.

<u>Table 4.</u> Frequency of ' cτ '-medials (' cτ ' preceded by a single symbol) showing total and line-initial frequencies.

<u>Table 5.</u> Biol. B line-initial frequencies (all 'words') plus frequencies of finals preceding the listed initials.

<u>Table 6.</u> Biol. B - Effect of final on initial of following 'word.'

(1)	(2)	(3)	(4)	(5)	(6)
1	A	1	2	1	
2	A	3	4		
3	A	5	6		
4	A	7	8		
5	A	9	10		
6	A	11	12		
7	A	13	14		
8	A	15	16		
9	A	17	18		
10	A	19	20		
11	A	21	22		
12	X	X	X		
13	A	23	24		
14	A	25	26		
15	A	27	28		
16	A	29	30		
17	A	31	32		
18	A	33	34		
19	A	35	36		
20	A	37	38		
21	A	39	40		
22	A	41	42		
23	A	43	44		
24	A	45	46		
25	A	47	48		

(1)	(2)	(3)	(4)	(5)
26	B	49	50	2
27	A	51	52	1
28	A	53	54	1
29	A	55	56	1
30	A	57	58	1
31	B	59	60	2
32	A	61	62	1
33	B	63	64	2
34	B	65	66	2
35	A	67	68	1
36	A	69	70	1
37	A	71	72	1
38	A	73	74	1
39	B	75	76	2
40	B	77	78	2
41	B	79	80	2
42	A	81	82	1
43	B	83	84	2
44	A	85	86	1
45	A	87	88	1
46	B	89	90	2
47	A	91	92	1
48	B	93	94	2
49	A	95	96	1
50	B	97	98	2

(1)	(2)	(3)	(4)	(5)
51	A	99	100	1
52	A	101	102	1
53	A	103	104	1
54	A	105	106	1
55	B	107	108	2
56	A	109	110	1
57	B	111	112	2
58	A	113	114	
59	X	X	X	
60	X	X	X	
61	X	X	X	
62	X	X	X	
63	X	X	X	
64	X	X	X	
65		115	116	
66	B	117	118	
67		119	120	
68				
69				
70	X	X	X	
71				
72				
73				
74			7146	
75	B	147	148	2

(1)	(2)	(3)	(4)	(5)
76	B	149	150	2
77	B	151	152	2
78	B	153	154	2
79	B	155	156	2
80	B	157	158	2
81	B	159	160	2
82	B	161	162	2
83	B	163	164	2
84	B	165	166	2
85	B	167 168 169	170 171 172	3
86	B	173 174 175	176 177 178	3
87	A	179	180	4
88	A	181	182	4
89	A	183 184	185 186	
90	A	187 188	189 190	
91	X	X	X	
92	X	X	X	
93	A	191	192	4
94	B	193	194	5
95	B	195 196	197 198	5
96	A	199	200	4
97	X	X	X	
98	X	X	X	
99	A	201	202	4?
100	A	203	204	4?

(1)	(2)	(3)	(4)	(5)
101	A	205 206	207 208	4?
102	A	209 210	211 [212]	
103	B	213	214	X
104	B	215	216	X
105	B	217	218	Y
106	B	219	220	X
107	B	221	222	
108	B	223	224	
109	X	X	X	
110	X	X	X	
111	B	225	226	
112	B	227	228	
113	B	229	230	
114	B	231	232	
115	B	[illegible]	[illegible]	
116	B	235	236	

VOYNICH MS PAGINATION

(1) FOLIO
(2) 'LANGUAGE'
(3) (4) Page
(5) Hand

TABLE A

	HERB A	PHAR A	HERB B	PHAR B	BIOL B	REC.	ASTRO
cc9P	118 3	50 -	119 -	27 -	81 1	NL -	92
cco9P	212 26	58 2	5 -	18 -	3 -	124 2	73
ct9P	24 -	13 -	38 1	16 -	67 -	58 1	25
cto9P	45 10	16 -	4 1	7 1	5 -	39 2	14
4o9P	496 144	344 21	212 18	261 10	1359 156	1556 49	55
o9P	651 104	392 20	377 11	313 5	666 19	1669 61	801
99P	298 51	97 28	171 42	153 20	71 19	171 39	148
89P	3 -	6 -	9 2	25 1	56 -	371 3	2
or9P	8 -	11 1	29 1	76 4	153 7	115 19	9
49P	2 -	27 -	- -	- -	6 -	3 -	2
4or9P	- -	- -	1 -	- -	30 -	84 -	
or9P	- -	- -	- -	6 -	- -	31 -	
8o9P	- -	- -	- -	- -	2 -	11 -	
4c9P	- -	- -	5 -	- -	10 -	2 -	
9P	207 37	69 43	96 58	95 32	136 49	746 102	46
8P	39 27	32 20	50 35	39 28	93 71	221 162	9
IP	263 18	69 18	110 6	42 5	103 5	262 18	27
-P	26 4	5 1	11 -	4 -	6 -	35 12	-
Wds.	c.6500	c.2900	2700	c 2200	6500	11000	
LINES	1085	c.360	315	c.220	780	1076	—

	HERB A	PHAR A	HERB B	PHAR B	BIOL B	REC	ASTRO
ccHP	76 1	20 -	63 -	29 -	146 1	167 -	10
ccoHP	33 1	28 -	7 -	3 -	- -	31 1	15
ctHP	17 1	6 1	4 -	6 -	108 1	58 -	4
ctoHP	11 -	19 3	12 1	4 -	2 1	9 -	2
4oHP	23 1	36 1	3 -	4 -	9 -	17 -	3
oHP	19 1	15 2	16 -	9 2	7 -	15 -	23
9HP	6 1	1 -	1 —	- -	1 1	- -	-
8HP	- -	- -	- -	- -	- -	- -	-
o8HP	- -	- -	- -	- -	- -	- -	-
4HP	- -	- -	5 -	2 -	10 -	6 -	—
HP	326 3	80 -	19 -	2 -	19 -	15 3	13 -
HP	67 1	15 -	7 -	4 -	87 -	15 -	3 -
HP	82 -	59 -	14 -	- -	7 -	9 -	7 -
HP	14 -	6 -	3 -	1 -	2 -	1 -	- -

TABLE 1

FREQUENCY OF INITIALS WITH MEDIAL (9P, IP, 8P, -P) and (HP, HP, HP, HP)
Total in col 1, line initial in col. 2

		9	8g	o8g	oR	aP	aiP	au	aiu	aiu	quw	aH	oR	aP	aiu	aH	8	Z	8	8a	o	o8	o8a	oZ	cg	oa
HERB A 6500	cc	585	15	84	33	64	4	(17)	26	(78)	·	19	554	440	(22)	27	10	6	1	3	73	28	71	28	18	12
	ct	268	1	15	7	24	·	4	3	(18)	·	2	58	67	·	·	·	21	·	·	21	6	16	6	1	·
PHAR A 2900	cc	34	9	39	1	7	·	·	1	·	·	·	129	70	·	3	1	7	1	1	23	8	34	33	3	·
	ct	127	7	67	5	·	·	·	·	·	·	1	117	80	·	12	·	10	·	1	34	7	15	28	6	·
HERB B 2700	cc	61	143	20	2	6	·	·	·	1	·	2	31	12	·	·	2	5	10	47	1	3	5	9	2	2
	ct	76	158	23	1	4	·	·	·	·	·	1	15	5	·	·	·	16	7	12	10	3	2	10	1	1
PHAR B 2200	cc	52	100	24	3	9	·	·	·	3	·	1	34	31	1	·	·	3	7	44	3	3	8	2	1	3
	ct	105	123	17	1	3	·	·	·	1	·	·	12	5	·	·	·	16	6	30	6	2	4	6	1	1
BIOL B 6500	cc	66	47	·	23	15	·	1	2	1	·	5	55	10	·	·	14	6	3	13	·	·	1	·	·	·
	ct	438	369	·	22	13	·	·	·	1	·	2	94	24	·	·	·	28	30	49	·	·	·	·	·	·
REC. 11000	cc	163	183	35	44	62	·	4	14	16	·	7	126	58	2	·	23	12	12	78	15	8	45	21	2	18
	ct	693	804	74	26	29	·	·	3	1	·	4	143	42	·	1	·	41	28	164	47	12	58	31	5	22
ASTRO	cc	73	20	11	16	12	·	·	·	2	·	4	58	13	·	·	4	12	·	11	13	·	8	5	1	4
	ct	111	34	24	6	4	·	·	·	·	·	·	30	17	·	·	·	34	1	14	10	·	12	12	2	1

TABLE 2.

FREQUENCY OF FINALS FOLLOWING cc/ct both INITIAL AND MEDIAL

FREQ. OF FINALS FOLLOWING MEDIAL ¶, 卄

HERB A – 6500 wd
BIOL B – 6500 wd
HERB B – 2700 wd

TABLE 3

Medial	Source	9 c9 cc9 8 9 c8 9 cc8 9 o8 9 co8 9	ox oT aiT av aiv aiiv aiiiv aiiv	ox cox oT coT aiiv oiiv	8 c2 cc2 8 c8 8a c8a	o8 c8a oT o9 o co CT	Tot
4o¶	HERB A	53 10 24 1 - - 4 -	6 8 1 1 28 5	46 8 29 3 8 2	- - 2 - - - - -	5 1 - 1	227/493
	BIOL B	92 49 96 - 209 194 2 -	154 65 2 175 100 4	30 3 5 4 - -	7 2 2 - 12 - 7	- - - - - -	57,350
	HERB B	8 3 7 2 47 13 4 6	14 22 1 4 11 2	7 3 1 1	1 2 2 6	1 2	28
o¶	HERB A	41 4 11 2 - 1 3 2	32 12 3 6 63 1 13	58 13 30 7 4 3	2 1	3 3 2 2 3	453/648
	BIOL B	33 24 34 - 96 60 - 1	60 47 3 68 46 1	21 16 4 - - -	3 - 12	- - - - -	42,606
	HERB B	23 8 11 - 44 13 2 11	34 48 6 11 29 18	13 10 6 5	1 3 3 7	2 2 4 1 3	45
9¶	HERB A	31 3 11 - - - 2 2	6 4 3 1 2 22 5	23 1 16 2 6 -	- 1 - - -	1 3 1 3	122/148
	BIOL B	1 1 12 - 14 13 - -	4 2 - 5 4 - 1	1 - - - - -			5 11
	HERB B	6 6 15 1 23 15 7	6 14 6 3 9 1 5	2 4 2	1 1	2 2 3	32
x¶	HERB A	- - - - - - 1 -	- - - - - - -	- - - - - -	- - - - - -	- - - - - -	5 6
	BIOL B	3 1 3 - 10 8 - -	1 6 6 5 1	1 1	2 1	1	56
	HERB B						
ox¶	HERB A	- - - - - - - -	- - - - - - - -	- - - - - - -	- - - - - - -	- - - - - - -	8
	BIOL B	12 6 23 - 23 20 - -	7 7 2 27 12 1 2	2 1 1 - 1 -	1 1		153
	HERB B						
cc¶	HERB A	30 2 4 - - - 5 -	3 6 1 1 2 12 1 - -	9 - 5 - 1 1	- - 1	1 1 1 1	37 118
	BIOL B	13 13 2 - 11 2 - -	5 6 1 1 10 2 - -	5 1 - -			9
	HERB B						
cco¶	HERB A	51 4 9 - - - 3 4	2 2 1 2 3 14 - 2	16 4 9 3 1 -	2	1 1 4	70 214
	BIOL B	4 - -					8
	HERB B						
cc卄	HERB A	49 1 1 - - - 2 -	5 1 1 - -	5 4		2	93
	BIOL B	144 30 - 11 18 - - -	3	1	1 1		244
	HERB B						
cco卄	HERB A	34 4 - - - - 1 -	2 1	2 1			44
	BIOL B	1 1 - - - - - -					2
	HERB B						
4o卄	HERB A	11 3 - - - - -					23
	BIOL B						9
	HERB B						
o卄	HERB A	7 - - - - - 3 -	1 1 2	1 3		1 1 1 -	19
	BIOL B						1
	HERB B						

	HERBAL A		HERBAL B		BIOLOGICAL B		RECIPES		PHARMACEUTICAL A	
4ocz	11	6	—	—	3	—	12	2	2	—
ocz	38	24	4	—	9	5	34	17	4	3
9cz	78	65	16	10	40	33	124	112	31	28
8cz	43	63	21	15	64	48	68	61	34	23
2cz	33	16	4	1	26	14	10	10	13	3
Rcz	7	4	13	7	185	17	203	7	3	—
o8cz	17	4	17	3	118	12	70	19	22	—
4o8cz	—	—	—	—	50	2	5	—	1	—
Pcz	7	—	2		31	—	17	—	1	—
oPcz	22	13	1	—	7	—	13	6	2	—
4Pcz	115	40	34	23	36	22	79	53	16	9
Fcz	45	31	30	21	47	27	115	74	17	10
HPcz	136	23	22	4	14	—	49	9	8	2
Fcz	18	9	10	—	6	2	26	7	3	—
Words	6500		2700		6500		11000			
Lines	1085		315		740		1076			
L/W	1/6		1/9		1/9		1/10			

TABLE 4

FREQUENCIES OF cz/cz MEDIALS SHOWING (1) TOTAL AND (2) LINE-INITIAL COUNTS

Note The Word/Line ratio is a rough approximation of the percentage of the total frequency expected in line-initial position.

(1)	Tot	L.I. (740)	9 (2800)	iiv (900)	x (900)	P (500)	(2)	Tot	L.I. (740)	9 (2800)	iiv (900)	x (900)	P (500)	(3)	Tot	L.I. (740)	9 (2800)	iiv (900)	x (900)	P (500)	(4)	Tot	L.I. (740)	9 (2800)	iiv (900)	x (900)	P (500)
cc	464	10	114	124	149	55	cc4P	81	1	28	32	8	8								ccdh	141	1	40	59	20	26
co	68	5	26	11	17	6	co4P	3	.	2	1										codh	-	-	-	-	-	-
ćc	446	16	101	110	127	92	ćc4P	67	-	18	26	8	12								ćcdh	103	-	31	36	17	16
ćo	64	6	19	20	8	8	ćo4P	6	1	4	-	-	1								ćodh	2	1	-	-	-	-
4o	49	10	35	-	2	-	4o4P	1359	156	1062	31	76	21	4occ	3	-	3	-	-	-	4odh	9	3	4	-	1	-
o	35	6	6	10	8	5	o4P	666	19	320	130	78	65	occ	9	5	2	-	-	2	odh	7	-				
g	20	4	3	8	2	3	g4P	71	19	24	7	2	7	gcc	40	33	2	-	4	1	gdh	1	1	-	-	-	-
8	385	57	192	40	83	12	84P	7	-	5	1	-	1	8cc	64	48	11	-	3	1							
2	250	124	78	10	21	4	24P	5	-	3	1	1	-	2cc	26	14	11	-	2	-							
x	112	8	94	4	6	1	x4P	56	-	46	-	10		xcc	185	17	144	-	14	-							
ox	290	4	71	74	53	53	ox4P	153	7	52	36	21	28	oxcc	118	12	48	18	24	12							
4ox	106	13	85	1	10	-	4ox4P	31	2	25	3	-	-	4oxcc	52	2	40	4	4	1							
P	92		74	2	12	1	P4P	1						Pcc	37	-	34	-	3	-							
oP	102	3	28	11	23	18	oP4P							oPcc	7	-	6	-	1	-							
4P	100	28	46	1	21	-								4Pcc	36	22	7	-	5	1							
4P'	46	45	1	-	-	-								4P'cc	47	27	15	-	5	-							
HP	81	5	36	2	39	3								HPcc	14	-	9	-	4	1							
FP	-	-	-	-	-	-								FPcc	6	2	-	-									
4Pdh	17	2	9	3	2	1																					
4P'dh	7	1	2	2	1	1																					
HPdh	7	1	2	2	1	1																					
FPdh	2	-	-	1	-	1																					

BIOL. B (pp 147-166) (740 lines, 6500 wds. = 9 w/L)

(a) Line-initial frequencies, (b) Frequency of finals (9 (9, 89, o89); iiv (aiiv, aiiiv, oiiiv, oiiv) x (ax, aix, ox, x); P (aP, aiP, oP) preceding the initials listed in cols 1, 2, 3, 4.

Col 1 = all occurences not included in Cols. 2, 3 + 4.

Col 2 = medial 4P (= 4P, 4P', HP, FP)

Col 3 = medial cc (= cc, ćc)

Col 4 = medial cdh (= 4Pdh, 4P'dh, HPdh, FPdh)

Figures above L.I. = number of lines in the BIOL. B section; above the four finals (9, iiv, x, P) = total frequency of each in final position.

TABLE 5

	line final	Preceding words with initial: 4o	o	g	8	2	x	?	cc	ct	ox
4oHax		6	6	–	17	2	2	–	24	22	
4oPax	1	2	1	1	4	1	–	–	6	2	
oHax	2	1	2	–	3	1	–	–	4	3	
oPax	3	2	4	–	1	–	–	–	6	5	
8ax	10	2	3	2	8	2	4	1	8	6	
2ax	3	–	1	–	2	–	–	–	3	4	
4oHa?		5	3	1	1	–	–	–	8	21	
4oPa?		–	2	1	–	1	–	–	4	2	
oHa?	–	2	5	–	–	–	–	–	4	4	
oPa?	1	–	3	1	3	–	–	–	5	1	
8a?	5	3	9	2	4	1	1	–	5	10	
2a?	4	–	–	–	–	1	1	–	1	3	
4oHaiv		7	26	–	14	1	–	–	42	30	
4oPaiv	1	–	4	–	–	1	–	–	11	3	
oHaiv	3	3	3	2	1	1	–	–	8	11	
oPaiv	1	–	8	1	–	–	–	–	4	5	
8aiv	2	1	6	–	4	1	–	–	14	6	
2aiv	2	1	4	–	–	–	–	–	3	7	
4oHaiiv	–	3	12	–	5	2	–	–	29	20	
4oPaiiv	1	3	–	–	–	1	–	–	6	2	
oHaiiv	3	1	6	–	3	–	–	–	8	5	
oPaiiv	–	–	3	–	–	–	–	–	2	3	
8aiiv	8	2	9	2	7	–	–	–	22	14	
2aiiv	3	2	1		2	2	–	–	9	11	
									236	2[illegible]	
4oHc8g	4	54	19	1	12	4	16	7	15	16	
4oPc8g	3	17	6	–	2	1	–	4	4	2	
oHc8g	1	11	8	1	5	1	6	2	1	4	
oPc8g	2	15	7	1	4	1	1	1	4	5	
ccc8g	11	86	19	1	13	6	13	3	13	10	
ctc8g	9	118	17	4	8	5	7	1	10	14	
4oHcc8g	3	70	15	2	7	2	16	6	11	6	
4oPcc8g	3	18	5	–	2	–	4	1	3	1	
oHcc8g	4	10	4	–	2	–	2	1	2	4	
oPcc8g	2	7	4	–	–	1	1	1	6	1	
cccc8g	2	11	1	–	–	1	4	–	1	–	
ctcc8g	–	20	3	–	1	–	4	4	2	2	
4oHcg	3	15	4	–	3	4	4	–	1	2	
4oPcg	–	4	2	–	–	–	1	–	–	–	
oHcg	1	3	1	–	2	–	3	–	1	–	
oPcg	–	2	3	–	1	–	2	–	1	1	
cccg	5	30	3	–	7	1	13	6	1	–	
ctcg	3	40	5	–	7	–	7	1	2	2	
4oHccg	3	20	16	1	6	–	13	9	6	2	
4oPccg	–	2	1	–	–	–	1	1	1	1	
oHccg	–	6	1	–	3	–	4	–	1	–	
oPccg	1	8	2	–	–	–	3	–	1	1	
ccccg	1	10	2	–	5	1	3	5	1	3	
ctccg	–	16	5	1	–	–	2	1	3	–	
									91	71	

BIOL B (pp 147-166) 760 lines, 6500 wds

EFFECT OF FINAL ON INITIAL 'LETTER' OF FOLLOWING 'WORD' IN BIOL B

Selected high frequency 'words' with x, ?, iiv, g finals showing that
(a) 'words' ending in x, ? and iiv are followed most frequently by 'words' with initial cc/ct and only rarely or not at all by 'words' with initial x or ?
(b) 'words' ending in g are followed most frequently by 'words' with initial 4o; and includes most 'words' with initial x or ?.

TABLE 6

APPENDIX B

What Constitutes Proof?

Stuart H. Buck

November 1976

I don't have any answers to offer - only a few questions and some observations. It seems to me that the main problem confronting anyone wishing to evaluate claims of a solution of the Voynich Manuscript is how to test the bits and scraps of decrypted text offered as proof. If a crib seems to work in one or two places, how can anyone determine that the <u>same</u> Voynich symbols always mean the <u>same thing</u> throughout the entire manuscript? There exists no standard index of the whole corpus showing every occurrence of each "character" with preceding and following context. If someone were to undertake to make such an index, how are the Voynich characters to be represented in Roman letters or other symbols that can be printed out by the computer? Is anyone certain how many basic or distinctive elements are contained in the script? How do these elements combine with each other? How should their ligatures be represented?

Furthermore, if someone offers a partial decryption in a language as it was presumed to be used in some period before the sixteenth century, what means do we have of testing the validity of a decryption in any of the languages of that period? For example, who has access to a plain language study of medieval Latin? What statistical knowledge do we have of other languages that might have been used? How can one determine the relative frequency of vocabulary, common stereotypes, clichés, etc.? Who today is steeped in the highly specialized vocabulary of alchemy, magic, astrology, cosmology, herbals, and other topics suggested by the drawings in the Voynich Manuscript? Or are these to be ignored? If so, why?

Perhaps the most serious problem confronting the student of the manuscript is lack of knowledge of its age and country of origin. The fact is, it cannot be traced beyond the court of Rudolph II of Bohemia - and how it got there is uncertain. And yet the identity of the author of the manuscript is all-important. One would not expect a man to devise such an elaborate scheme to hide a text in a language that he didn't know. It seems reasonable, then, to assume that the underlying language of the manuscript would be the one used by educated men in the country where the author resided. This does not have to he the case, but it is highly likely; if, indeed, a natural language is involved at all. Any hypothesis, then, that ignores any real knowledge of the age and place of origin of the manuscript is taking grave risks, and would require massive internal evidence in order to be acceptable.

One last word: if you think that the Voynich Manuscript is nothing but an elaborate hoax, then that also is a hypothesis to be demonstrated or disproved. You can't just wave the whole thing aside because you don't understand it. The Voynich Manuscript does not deserve our attention merely because it is an intriguing enigma demanding an answer only because it is there. What makes it worth talking about is that it involves questions of methodology, tools, and validation that concern all analysts faced with the problem of deciphering secret writing, past and present.

www.ingramcontent.com/pod-product-compliance
Lightning Source LLC
LaVergne TN
LVHW082034050326
832904LV00006B/282

* 9 7 8 1 6 0 8 8 8 1 7 3 4 *